Thomas Becket

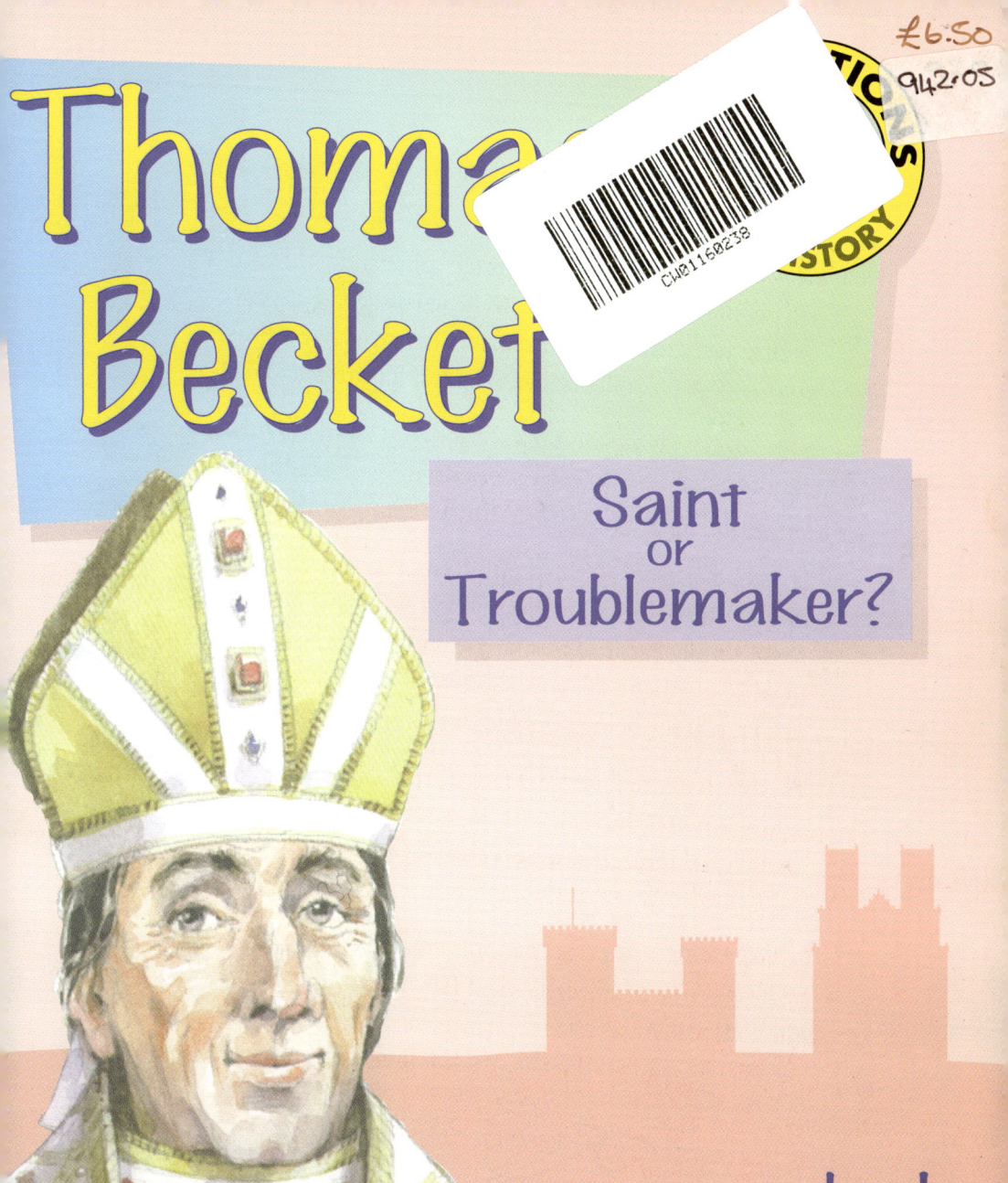

Saint or Troublemaker?

Josh Brooman

LONGMAN

To the reader

Many of us have a **reputation** for something. Do you? Do people say, for example, that you are good at sport, or that you are a brilliant dancer? Perhaps they admire your computer skills, or even your ability to tell jokes?

Some of us have a good reputation, but some do not. It's easy, for example, to get a reputation for always being late, or for talking too much, or for being mean.

Usually we deserve our reputations, but sometimes it can be unfair. People might say that you have no dress sense simply because they are jealous of the way you look. They might call you a show-off just because they dislike you for being popular.

History is a little like this. There are thousands of men and women in history who have reputations both good and bad. But do they deserve them? Have they been judged fairly?

This is what this book is about. It asks you to decide whether one of history's most famous saints, Thomas Becket, really was a saint. Or was he, as some people said at the time, a troublemaker who deserved a nasty end?

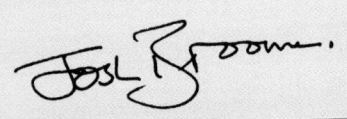

Contents

Introduction	4
Overview The English Church	8
1 Thomas Becket	10
Task How did Thomas become an important man?	15
Overview How the king governed	16
2 King Henry II	18
Task Why did Henry want to control the Church?	23
Overview The power of an archbishop	24
3 The quarrel	26
Task Why did Thomas and Henry quarrel?	33
4 Murder in the cathedral	34
Task Why do pictures of the murder tell different stories?	39
Overview Pilgrims, shrines and saints	40
5 The martyr and the miracles	42
Task Miracles or make-believe?	47
You decide – saint or troublemaker?	48

Introduction

The rider was tired. He had been in the saddle for four days. He had eaten nothing but bread and he had drunk only water. Now, from the top of a hill, he could see the end of his journey only a few miles away – the cathedral in the city of Canterbury.

But he did not spur his horse to finish the journey quickly. He dismounted, took off his clothes and shoes, and put on a shirt lined with stiff, prickly hair. Then, leaving his horse, he began walking barefoot into the city.

The road was rough and stony, and his feet were soon bleeding. As he entered the cathedral he left footprints of blood behind him. Painfully, he walked downstairs into the crypt, a burial place beneath the cathedral floor. There, he knelt before the tomb of a man who had been murdered several years before, and wept.

As he did so, eighty monks filed into the crypt behind him. Each was carrying a whip. The man took off his hair shirt and, one by one, the monks whipped his bare back with three lashes each.

When they had finished, the man dressed and stayed the rest of the night alone in the dark, cold crypt. He left the cathedral early in the morning, taking with him some small bottles of holy water, mixed with blood from the body in the tomb.

The man's name was Henry, and he was the King of England. The body was that of Thomas Becket. The year was 1174.

Henry's journey, or pilgrimage, to Canterbury was not at all unusual. Hundreds of pilgrims visited Thomas Becket's tomb every day. Some went barefoot, or even on their knees. Some were whipped by monks. Others gave away large sums of money.

Ever since then, Thomas Becket has been one of the most famous people in history. Even in our own times, schools and streets have been named after him. Plays have been written, music has been composed, and films have been made about his life.

Why has he had such a remarkable reputation for over 800 years? Does he deserve that reputation? It is for you to decide after reading this book.

This stained glass window in Canterbury Cathedral shows King Henry praying at the tomb of Thomas Becket in 1174.

The English Church

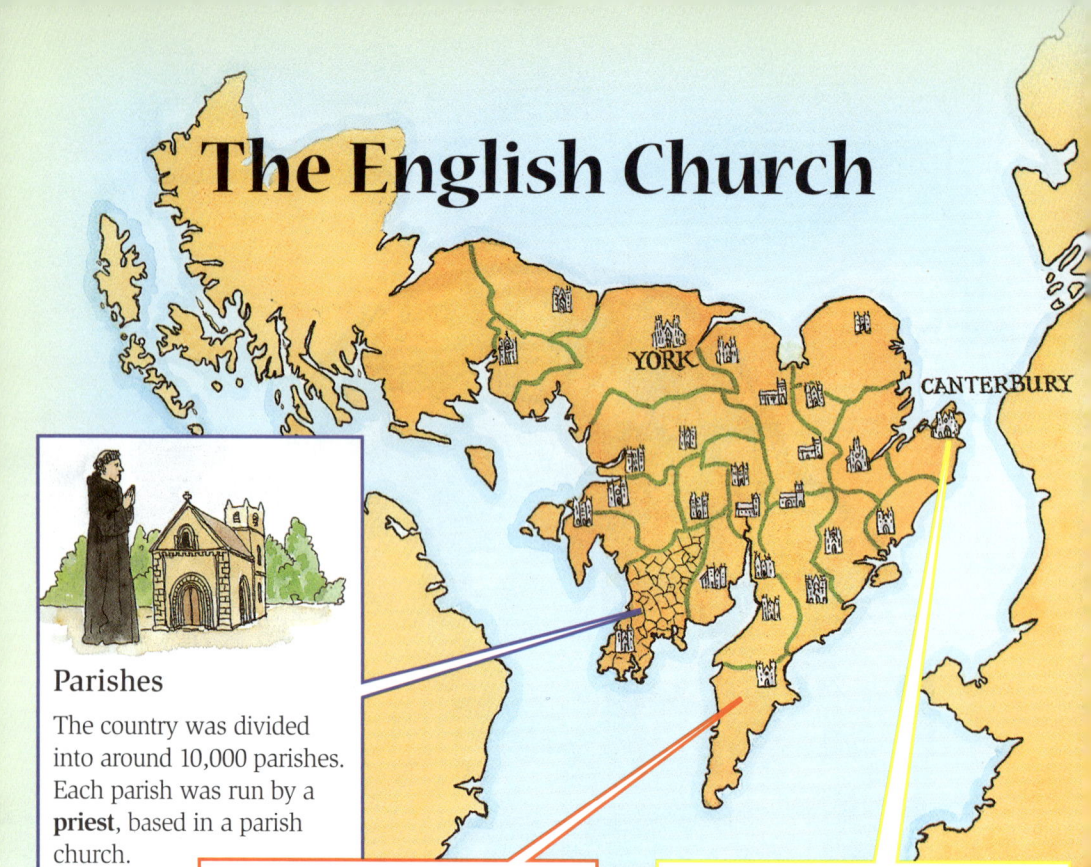

Parishes

The country was divided into around 10,000 parishes. Each parish was run by a **priest**, based in a parish church.

Dioceses

The parishes were grouped into 21 dioceses. Each diocese was run by a **bishop**.

Each bishop was based in a **cathedral**, a large church where he had his throne, or *cathedra*.

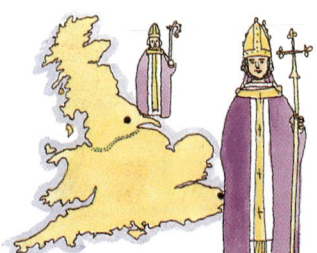

Provinces

The dioceses belonged to two provinces, Canterbury and York. Each was run by an **archbishop**. The Archbishop of Canterbury was the more powerful of the two.

8

The Church was the largest and most powerful organisation in England. Many thousands of people worked for it (the **clergy**). It had its own language (Latin) and its own law (**canon law**). It had branches in every part of the country and it owned one-third of all the land in England.

ROME

Monastic houses
About 5,000 of the clergy were monks, nuns, friars or canons. They lived by strict rules in 300 **monastic houses** (**monasteries, nunneries, abbeys**).

The Pope
The English Church was just one of many churches in Europe. At the head of them all was the **Pope** who was based in Rome.

Chapter 1

Thomas Becket

Thomas Becket became world-famous after he was horribly murdered. As you will read, four knights hacked his brains out in Canterbury Cathedral in the year 1170.

But Thomas was already famous years before his death. What was he famous for, and how had he become so important?

A Norman Londoner

Thomas Becket was born in London in 1118. This was just over 50 years after the Normans conquered Britain in 1066, and his parents were settlers from Normandy. So, although Thomas was a Londoner, he grew up speaking French.

If his family had been English, Thomas may not have become famous. At that time, Normans owned nearly all the land in the country, and they had more money and more power than the English. As one Englishman put it, 'the Normans are the high men and the low men are the English.'

A merchant's son

Thomas's father was a merchant. It was common at that time for sons to follow their fathers into business, without going to school. But Thomas did not do this. His mother wanted him to have an education. She sent him to a series of schools, where he learned to speak, read and write in Latin. This was the language used by lawyers and churchmen.

Merchants like Thomas's father were important men in society, but there were others who were more important. Noblemen such as barons had the highest rank in society. Thomas's father liked to entertain such men in his house. In this way, Thomas came to meet people of power and importance.

Powerful friends

One of these was Richer De Laigle, Lord of Pevensey Castle. Although he was some years older than Thomas, they became good friends. Richer often invited Thomas for holidays at Pevensey Castle. There he taught Thomas how to hunt with hawks and dogs. In Richer's company, Thomas learned how to behave like a nobleman.

Making an impression

Thomas was very tall by the time he left school. One record says that he was 6 feet and 11 inches tall (2.18 metres). He was also very thin. He had black hair, bright eyes and a big, hooked nose. Although he stammered slightly, people said that he had a pleasant voice. They found him intelligent, quick and witty.

With his striking looks, noble manners, and educated talk, Thomas made a strong impression on the people who met him. One of these was Theobald, the Archbishop of Canterbury. Theobald was always on the lookout for bright young men to work for him. He invited Thomas to live and work in his household.

For the next ten years Thomas worked for Theobald, who trained him in law and religion. He was so good at his work that Theobald made him his Archdeacon, or second-in-command, when he was only 35 years old.

Thomas had been Archdeacon for only a few weeks when the King died. This was a stroke of luck for Thomas. The new King, Henry II, wanted different people to work for him. He asked Theobald to suggest who should be his Chancellor, and Theobald gave him Thomas's name. Thomas became Chancellor in 1155, aged 36.

Thomas the Chancellor

The Chancellor was the King's closest adviser. He went everywhere with the King, advising him at all times. He dealt with the King's letters, stamping them with a huge seal made of red wax to show that they were genuine. And he kept the records of the King's finances.

Thomas earned a great deal of money as Chancellor. He

spent much of it on luxuries. He dressed in clothes made of silk and fur, and rode on horses harnessed with silver. Also, he was generous with his money. He showered his friends with gifts. Almost every day he welcomed large numbers of guests into his house. They ate from silver plates and drank fine wines from golden cups. Minstrels and acrobats entertained them while they feasted.

But Thomas was not a greedy man. He ate simple food and drank herb tea rather than wine. He was much cleaner than many people were at that time. He liked to wash in scented water, and he had fresh rushes spread on his floors every day.

King's friend as well as Chancellor

Although Thomas was 36 years old, and King Henry was 22, the two men got on so well that they became good friends. They went hunting, hawking and riding together, and they played each other at chess, gambling on who would win.

Thomas also worked hard as Chancellor, helping Henry to do all the things a King had to do. He helped Henry to run the government. He helped him to get rid of rivals and enemies, and he arranged agreements with the rulers of foreign countries. He even helped Henry to fight wars. In 1159 he led 700 knights into battle against the King of France, fighting and killing as if he were a soldier.

This stained glass window in Canterbury Cathedral shows Thomas Becket as Archbishop of Canterbury. He is sitting on the Archbishop's throne, or cathedra. He is holding a Bible in one hand and pointing to heaven with the other. The hat he is wearing is a mitre.

Thomas becomes Archbishop of Canterbury

Thomas was the King's closest adviser, but another man was even more important: Theobald, the Archbishop of Canterbury. In 1161, however, Theobald died.

Theobald had helped Henry in many ways, and Henry was grateful for this. But he felt that the Archbishop of Canterbury had too much power. He wanted the next Archbishop to share control of the Church with him. It seemed to him that the obvious man to do this was his friend and Chancellor, Thomas Becket. Thomas became Archbishop in 1162.

Task: how did Thomas become an important man?

Look at the picture opposite. Now think of yourself as a maker of stained glass windows in 1162. You have to make three more windows, showing important times in Thomas's life before he became Archbishop of Canterbury.

1 Choose from pages 10–15 what you think were the three most important times in his life. Then describe or sketch what each window would show.

2 Was there anything bad about Thomas that you would *not* show?

How the king governed

The king
Henry was King of England, Duke of Normandy, Count of Anjou and Duke of Aquitaine. He was, therefore, the ruler of a huge empire. He spent much of his time travelling around his empire, keeping order and judging legal cases.

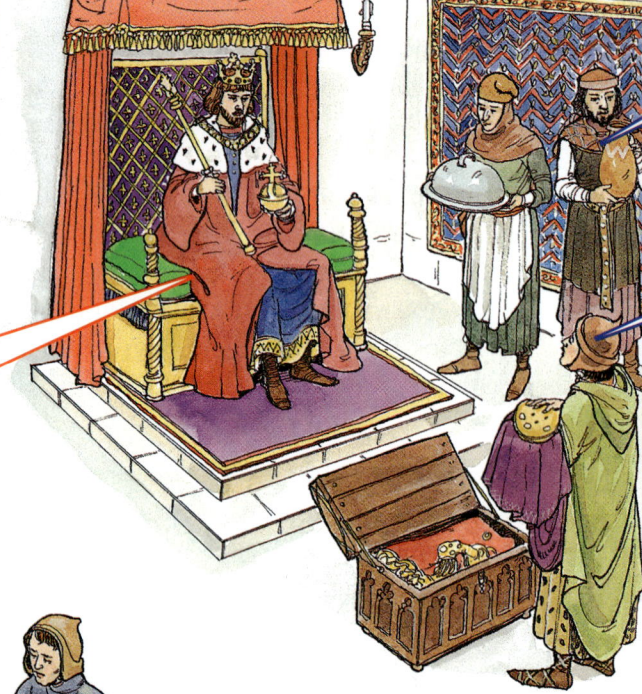

The Exchequer
This was the department which looked after the king's finances. The Treasurer worked out how much tax each sheriff must pay to the king. He worked out the sums on a chequered cloth, which is why this department was called the Exchequer.

The king's household
Four officials advised the king and looked after his needs.

His **Steward** ran the **Hall** – the cooks and servants who provided food and drink for everyone in the household (about 300 people).

His **Marshal** ran the **Constabulary** – the horsemen who organised all the king's travel arrangements.

His **Chamberlain** ran the **Chamber** – the servants who looked after the king's clothes, jewels and money.

His **Chancellor** ran the **Chancery** – the clerks who kept written records of all the king's business.

Sheriffs
A sheriff ran each shire. He collected taxes and rents for the king. He carried out orders sent to him by the king. He made sure that people in the shire had weapons to help defend the country. He held a law court in each district, or **hundred**, of the shire.

Chapter 2

King Henry II

What sort of person was King Henry? Why did he want more control over the Church?

Two of a kind?

Henry was unlike Thomas in almost every way. For a start, he was much younger than Thomas. When he became King, Henry was 21 years old and Thomas was aged 35.

The two men were very different to look at. Thomas was tall and elegant while Henry was short and muscular. Thomas had long, black hair, pale skin and blue eyes, while Henry had short red hair, a freckled face, and grey eyes. Thomas dressed in fine clothes and washed in scented water, while Henry often wore muddy riding clothes, and had dirty hands. Thomas had a pleasant voice and made polite conversation; Henry had a harsh voice, and often swore.

They did have some things in common. Both were educated men. Like Thomas, Henry could speak three languages – French, Latin and English. Above all, both were keen hunters. Henry enjoyed spending whole days on horseback, hunting with dogs or hawks.

Henry inherits 'a land full of castles'

When Henry became King in 1154, England was in a bad way. For the past twenty years, King Stephen had fought a war against his rival, Matilda. During the war, noblemen known as 'robber barons' took control of large parts of the country. A writer of the time described the results:

> *The barons filled the land full of castles. And when the castles were built, they took men and women prisoner, and tortured them to get their gold and silver. Some they hanged up by the feet and smoked them with foul smoke; some they hanged by the thumbs; others by the head, and hung burning things on their feet. Some they thrust into dungeons with adders and snakes…*
>
> *They were constantly taking money from the towns, and when the wretched men had no more to give, they destroyed and burnt the towns. Corn was expensive and there was no meat, cheese or butter in the land.*
>
> *They spared not even churches or churchyards, but stole anything that was valuable from them and then burnt the churches.*
>
> *Men openly said that Christ and his saints were asleep.*

Adapted from *The Anglo-Saxon Chronicle*, 1137

Henry restores law and order

When Henry became King at the end of the war, he needed to gain control of his country.

He began by destroying the castles of the robber barons. Then he made changes to the law. During the war the barons had set up their own law courts to try wrongdoers. Henry forbade the barons to have their own courts. Instead, he sent judges around the country to try cases before juries of twelve people. Gradually, these 'circuit judges' brought the King's justice to all parts of England.

Henry made changes to the way in which he governed the country. The picture on pages 16–17 shows how he governed. Before long, most people came to accept that England now had a strong king who meant to rule them firmly.

'Benefit of clergy'

But there was still one area in which Henry did not have complete power: the Church. In several important ways, the Church had the right to run its own affairs. One of these was the right to hold its own law courts. The law said that any member of the clergy accused of a serious crime could be tried only in a church court. This was known as 'benefit of clergy'.

Henry wanted to change this. Crimes by the clergy were increasing. During the first ten years of his reign more than a hundred murders were committed by clergy. There were also many cases of robbery, blackmail and even rape. Yet the church courts were much less severe than the royal courts. While a murderer might be sentenced to death in a royal court, a church court might only sack him from his job.

Henry thought that this was not enough to stop clergy from committing crimes. He wanted the church courts to send offenders to his own courts where they would be punished more severely. Moreover, many of these people were not even real clergy. Some pretended to be priests by shaving their heads so that they could be tried in church courts.

Henry hopes to avoid a quarrel

Although he was King, Henry could not easily change the system of 'benefit of clergy'. As you have read, the Church was a powerful organisation, led by the Archbishop of Canterbury and by the Pope. They wanted to control everything that went on in the Church, and they had often quarrelled with kings who tried to take away part of their power. Henry knew that he would start another argument if he did anything against the church courts.

'Benefit of clergy'. This painting shows a monk (on the left) and a nun (on the right) who have been found guilty of breaking their holy vows by having an affair. The church court which tried them has sentenced them to spend a day sitting in the stocks. This was an unpleasant punishment, as people like the man on the right gathered to make fun of the victims, but it was not as bad as some of the punishments given out by the royal courts.

This is why he wanted Thomas Becket to become Archbishop of Canterbury after Theobold's death in 1161. With his old friend as Archbishop as well as Chancellor, Henry thought there would be nobody to stop him making the changes he wanted.

He had no reason to suspect that this would quickly lead to one of the most violent disagreements in history.

Task: why did Henry want to control the Church?

King Henry was pleased when he made Thomas Becket Archbishop of Canterbury. He thought he could now control the Church. As if you are Henry, write a letter to Thomas telling him what you want him to do. In your letter:

a mention your old friendship and hunting together

b remind Thomas how he helped you to control the robber barons when he was Chancellor

c complain about 'benefit of clergy' and the softness of the church courts

d tell Thomas how he can help you to bring the Church under control.

The power of an archbishop

The archbishop...

... **crowned the king** and was **one of the king's most important advisers.**

... was **England's spiritual leader.** He tried to make sure that everybody in the country lived Christian lives.

... was **leader of the clergy.** He appointed bishops. He tried to make sure that all clergy lived holy lives and he punished those who failed to do so.

... was a **noble**. The greatest nobles regarded him as their equal.

... was a great **landowner**. The rent from his lands made him one of the richest men in the country.

... was a **law-giver**. He held courts in which he could try anybody who broke church rules. His strongest punishment was excommunication.

Excommunication was the banning of a wrongdoer from the Church. Someone who was excommunicated had no hope of going to heaven, and nobody was allowed to have anything to do with him. If he said he was sorry, the excommunication was lifted. If he died without saying sorry, he would go straight to hell.

Chapter 3

The quarrel

Soon after Thomas became Archbishop of Canterbury, people noticed a change in the way he behaved.

Every night, Thomas now got up from bed at midnight to go to Matins, the first church service of the day. Then he invited thirteen poor people into his home, washed their feet, fed them, and gave them money. Then he went back to bed for a few hours, getting up again at dawn to read the Bible.

Thomas's appearance also changed. He stopped wearing fashionable clothes, dressing instead in the black gown of a churchman. And although only his servant knew it, beneath his clothes Thomas wore a shirt lined with prickly goat hair that made his skin sore and itchy.

In short, Thomas had decided to live by strict religious rules and to punish himself every day.

'An unfriendly act'

At first, King Henry took little notice of this change in his friend's behaviour. Then he became angry. Shortly after becoming Archbishop, Thomas resigned as Chancellor. He told Henry that he simply didn't have time to do two such important jobs. Henry saw this as 'an unfriendly act'.

A year later, in 1163, they began to argue. They quarrelled over what to do with a priest accused of murder.

The case of Philip – priest and murderer

The priest's name was Philip. He had recently disagreed with a knight. When the knight was found dead, with a knife in his back, his family accused Philip of murder.

As you have read, priests accused of crimes were always tried in church courts. These were less strict than the royal courts. When Philip was tried by a church court, he was found innocent and set free.

One of the King's circuit judges was holding a court nearby when this happened. He decided that the case should not be closed, and ordered Philip to stand trial in the royal court. Philip lost his temper, refused the order, and hurled insults at the Judge.

King Henry was furious when he was told about this. But when he threatened Philip with death, Thomas Becket stepped in to protect Philip. He said that Philip could only be tried in a church court, and that he would try the case himself.

Thomas cleared Philip of the murder but found him guilty of insulting the King's judge. He sentenced him to be whipped, naked, in public. This was a harsher punishment than church courts usually gave, and Thomas hoped that it would satisfy Henry. But Henry was outraged. He thought Thomas had been too lenient. In his opinion, yet another criminal had escaped the death penalty simply because he was a priest.

The Clarendon Rules

The quarrel became much more serious in 1164. Henry summoned Thomas to a meeting at his hunting lodge at Clarendon. There he forced Thomas to sign a document known as the Clarendon Rules. The Rules gave Henry greater control over the Church, including the church courts. One rule said that priests must not speak to the Pope without the King's permission.

Thomas soon regretted signing the Rules. Without consulting Henry, he decided to go to Rome to discuss his worries with the Pope. Henry was furious when he heard of Thomas's plan, for his visit to the Pope would break the Clarendon Rules.

Henry decided that strong action was needed. He put Thomas on trial before a council of nobles in Northampton Castle. The nobles quickly decided that Thomas was guilty of treason – that he was a traitor to the King.

Thomas refused to accept their verdict. He said that he could only be tried in a church court, and walked out. As he left

This picture was painted in about 1130. It shows eight robbers being hanged for breaking into the abbey of Bury St Edmunds. This is the sort of punishment with which Henry threatened Philip, and from which Thomas tried to save him.

29

the council, the nobles shouted 'Traitor!' and threw rubbish from the floor at him.

Later that night, Thomas fled to the coast, and took a boat to France. He stayed there, in exile, for the next six years.

Exile

When Henry heard that Thomas had escaped, he ordered his roughest and nastiest knights, the Broc brothers, to take revenge against him. They confiscated all Thomas's land and belongings, and they made his relations, friends and servants leave the country. Hundreds of men, women and children were thrown out of their homes to join Thomas in exile.

As the years went by, Henry became less angry. Eventually, in 1170, he agreed to allow Thomas to return to England. However, before Thomas could return, a new quarrel flared up. This time it was over Henry's oldest son, who was also called Henry.

A royal coronation

Henry wanted his son to be crowned King while he himself was still alive. This would prevent any argument after his death about who should be king. However, kings could only be crowned by the Archbishop of Canterbury. As Thomas was still in exile, Henry ordered the Archbishop of York to crown his son instead.

This picture comes from a book about Thomas Becket's life, written about 50 years after his death. The picture shows two separate scenes. On the left is the coronation of the young King Henry in 1170. The Archbishop of York, helped by other bishops, has placed the crown on his head and put the royal sceptre into his hands. On the right of the picture is the coronation feast. King Henry II is giving his newly-crowned son a huge, golden cup. The writing underneath is in French, the language used at court at that time.

This was a challenge to Thomas's authority, and he decided to take action. Soon after returning to England he excommunicated the bishops who had taken part in the coronation. This was a terrible punishment, for it meant that they would go to hell if they did not repent before they died.

In revenge, the Broc family began to make life as hard as they could for Thomas. One of them captured the wagons bringing Thomas's belongings from France to Canterbury, and stole all his most valuable possessions. Another cut off the tail of one of Thomas's best horses. Thomas replied by excommunicating them too.

'This low-born priest'

The bishops complained bitterly to Henry, who was in France. One said, 'My Lord, while Thomas lives you will have no good days, nor quiet times, nor a peaceful kingdom.'

These words sent Henry into a fit of rage. He shouted, 'The man tramples on the whole royal family. What cowards do I have in my court, that not one will free me of this low-born priest.'

Four knights who heard those words decided to take action. Without telling Henry what they were doing, they slipped away from the court and crossed the Channel to England.

Task: why did Thomas and Henry quarrel?

1. With a partner, read the statements below. Decide which five statements Henry might have made, and which five Thomas might have made.

2. Use the statements to write a conversation between Henry and Thomas. Add details from pages 26–32 to make the conversation as realistic as you can.

- ◆ My nobles found you guilty of treason, but you refused to accept this and ran away to France.
- ◆ I didn't have time to do both jobs. All my time was taken up with religious life.
- ◆ You stopped my judge from punishing a murderer with death.
- ◆ When I let you return to England, you excommunicated three bishops.
- ◆ Philip was a priest. Only a church court has the right to try a priest.
- ◆ They threatened my authority. I had to deal firmly with them.
- ◆ I made you Archbishop as well as Chancellor so that you could help me control the Church. You let me down when you resigned as Chancellor.
- ◆ You signed the Clarendon Rules and then broke them by seeing the Pope without my permission.
- ◆ I am head of the Church. The nobles had no right to try me. Only a church court can try a churchman.
- ◆ You forced me to sign the rules. Anyway, I need to be in constant touch with the Pope. He is my religious leader.

Chapter 4

Murder in the cathedral

The four knights were experienced soldiers, but they were not ruffians. They were important and wealthy nobles in Henry's court. Their names were Hugh de Moreville, William de Tracy, Reginald FitzUrse and Richard le Breton.

After crossing the Channel, the four men rode to Saltwood Castle, home of the Broc brothers. There they spent the night making plans. On the 29th December, they galloped the last 24 kilometres to Canterbury. Riding behind them were the Brocs, leading a small army of soldiers.

The King commands...

At about three o'clock in the afternoon, the four knights entered the Archbishop's Hall, next to the cathedral. They were taken to see Thomas in his bedroom, where he was working with his clerks. They said to him: 'The King commands that you shall leave his realm.'

Thomas refused to move. The knights stormed out of the building, shouting 'To arms, to arms.' In the courtyard outside, they took off their cloaks and put on heavy armour: 20 kg coats of chain mail, and big steel helmets. From their scabbards they pulled razor-sharp swords a metre long.

As they were about to re-enter the building, two of Thomas's servants bolted the door shut. But some workmen had left their tools and a ladder lying on the ground nearby. One of the knights put the ladder up to the window and used a workman's axe to smash the shutter open. He climbed in, and unlocked the door for the others.

Thomas's clerks began to panic. Telling him that it was time for prayers, they hurried him out of his bedroom, through the cloisters and into the cathedral. They bolted the door behind them.

'Where is the traitor?'

Thomas ordered them to unlock the door, saying that a church is not a castle. Then he started to walk up the stairs to the choir. As he did so, the knights burst into the cathedral behind him. With their swords drawn they shouted, 'Where is the traitor? Where is Thomas Becket?'

By now, the short winter day was drawing in. The cathedral was lit only by candles, and Thomas could have slipped away easily into the darkness. Instead, he walked back down the steps and called out: 'Here I am. No traitor to the King but a priest of God. What do you want?'

Death in the dark

The knights rushed at him. One of them used the point of his sword to knock the mitre off Thomas's head. Then Reginald FitzUrse caught hold of his robes and tried to pull him out of the cathedral. But Thomas was a tall, strong man. He pushed FitzUrse away and sent him sprawling. Furious at being pushed over, FitzUrse sprang up and slashed at Thomas's head with his sword.

By this time, all but one of Thomas's servants had disappeared into the darkness to hide. His name was Edward Grim. Edward saw the blow coming, and raised an arm to ward it off. But the sword was heavy and sharp. It cut Edward's arm to the bone, then gashed open the skin on Thomas's bare head.

Thomas fell to his knees, then collapsed face down. As he lay there, William de Tracy sprang forward and sliced off the top of Thomas's skull. The blow was so hard that his sword broke in two on the stone floor. Finally, Hugh de Moreville trod hard on Thomas's neck, put the end of his sword into his open skull, and scattered his brains over the floor.

The time was half past four on 29th December, 1170.

The murder of Thomas Becket. This picture was painted in a prayer book about 50 years after Thomas's murder. It shows a series of events rather than a single moment in time. It starts with Thomas's mitre *(on the right of the picture) being knocked off, and ends with the fourth knight (second from the left) spilling his brains. Edward Grim is on the right of the picture.*

37

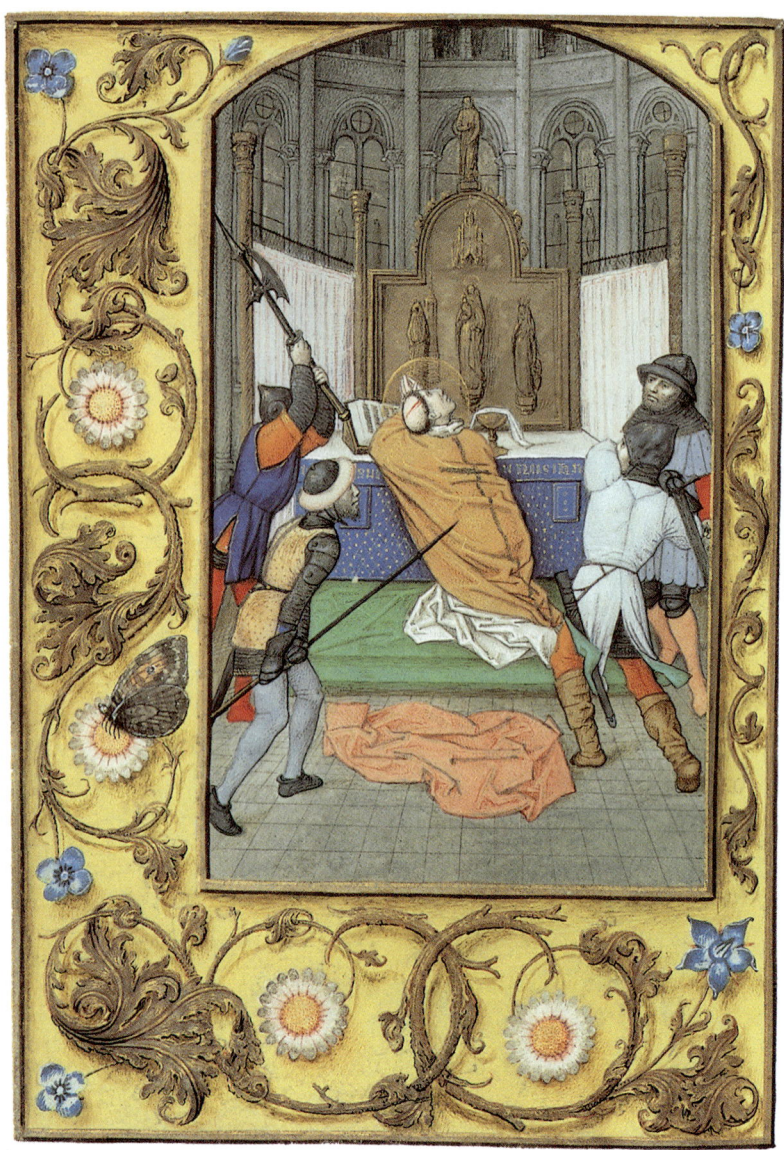

This picture was painted in about 1480, more than 300 years after Thomas's murder. Compare it with the picture on page 37 which was painted only 50 years afterwards.

Task: why do pictures of the murder tell different stories?

1 This is an outline of the picture on page 37. Make a copy of it. Then use page 36 to work out the order of the events shown in the picture. Write a sentence or two about each event in the boxes. One has been done as an example.

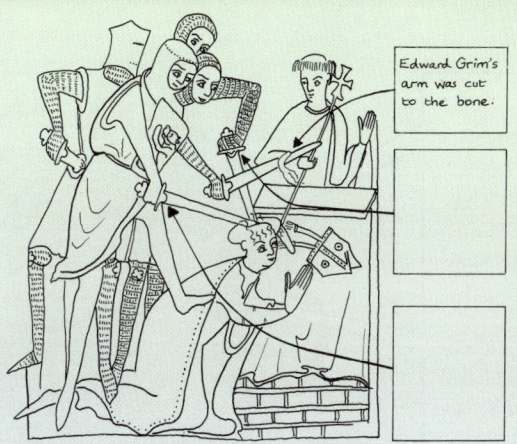

Edward Grim's arm was cut to the bone.

2 Compare your outline picture with the painting on page 38. The two pictures tell different stories.

   a Make a list of the differences between the two pictures.

   b Explain the differences, using these notes to help you:
   ◆ It was dark in the cathedral.
   ◆ All but one of Thomas's monks ran away to hide.
   ◆ One picture was painted 50 years after the murder, the other 300 years later.

   c Now explain which picture you think is the more accurate record of the murder.

Pilgrims, shrines and saints

A pilgrimage

Almost everybody in the Middle Ages went on a pilgrimage at least once in their lives. A pilgrimage was a journey to a shrine. Usually this was the burial place of a saint. Pilgrims visited shrines for many reasons. Some went to ask for the saint's help in curing an illness. Some went to give thanks for a happy event. Others went to ask the saint to forgive their sins.

A pilgrim

A badge to show where he had been, for example a badge of palm leaves if he had been to the Holy Land.

Woollen shirt, called a *sclavein*, tied at the waist with a belt.

Broad-brimmed hat for protection against sun and rain.

A bag called a *scrip*. This contained enough food and money to last for one day.

Strong boots and a long walking stick (as most pilgrims travelled on foot).

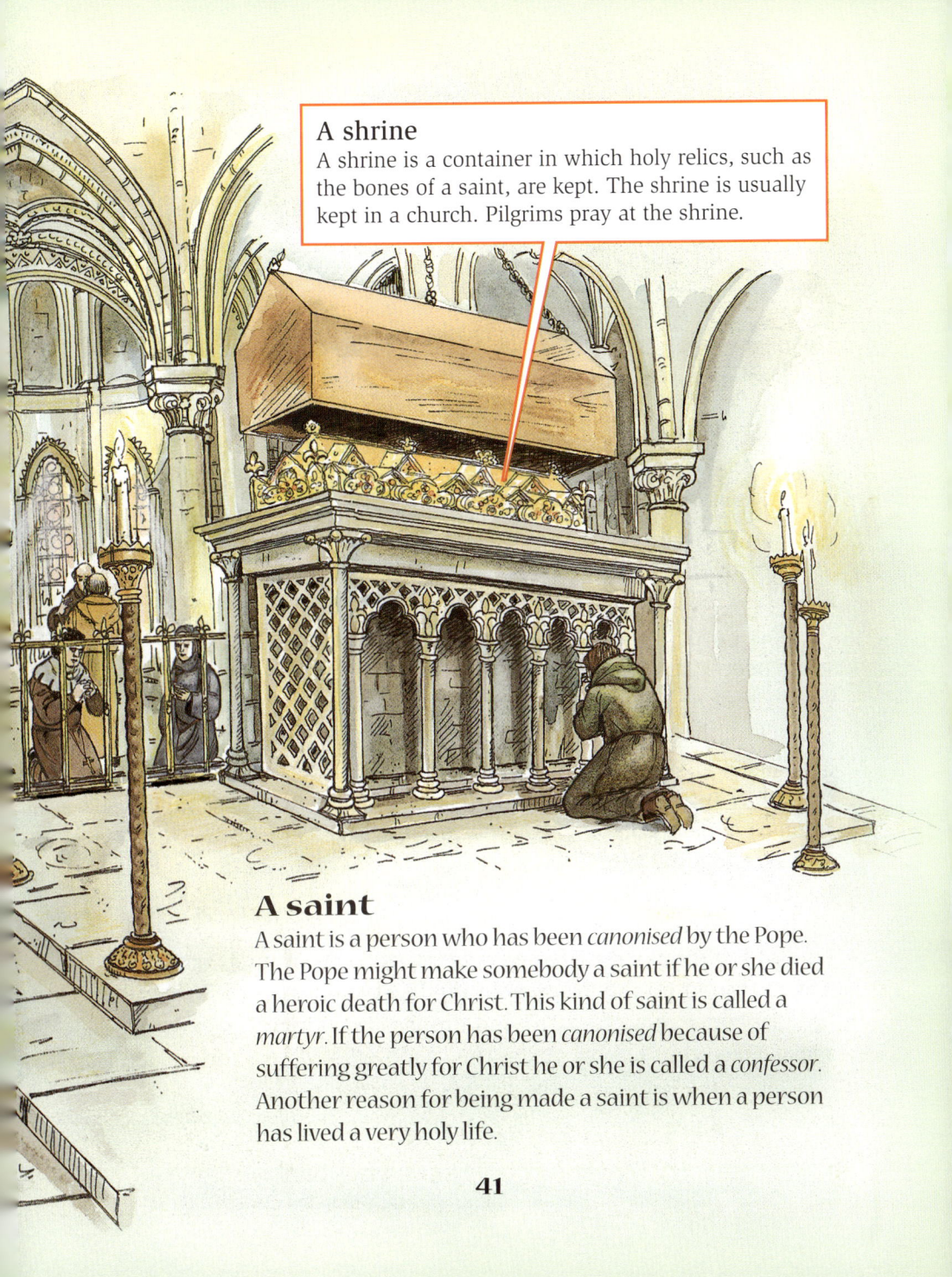

A shrine
A shrine is a container in which holy relics, such as the bones of a saint, are kept. The shrine is usually kept in a church. Pilgrims pray at the shrine.

A saint
A saint is a person who has been *canonised* by the Pope. The Pope might make somebody a saint if he or she died a heroic death for Christ. This kind of saint is called a *martyr*. If the person has been *canonised* because of suffering greatly for Christ he or she is called a *confessor*. Another reason for being made a saint is when a person has lived a very holy life.

Chapter 5

The martyr and the miracles

For a while, Thomas's body lay where he had fallen, in a pool of blood and brains.

Gradually, the monks came forward from their hiding places. Some whispered that Thomas had deserved his fate. They said that he had brought it upon himself by being so stubborn. Others were more respectful, and quietly prepared him for burial.

They cut away his bloodstained clothes, and gave them to poor people in the cathedral. Beneath these clothes, they found that he was wearing a hair shirt next to his skin. None of them had known that Thomas had been wearing this for years. They were even more amazed when they saw that the hair shirt was alive with lice and worms. Thomas must have been in constant agony. The monks saw this as proof that he had lived a holy life. They kissed his hands and feet and called him 'Saint Thomas'.

One of the monks now led a group back to the murder scene. They scraped up the remains of the blood and brains. Townspeople came forward and dipped their fingers into the mess. One went home, mixed the blood with water, and gave it to his wife who was immediately cured of a serious illness.

News of these events spread fast. As the news spread, it seemed that miracles took place. Thomas died on Tuesday, 29th December. On Thursday, a woman in Sussex was cured of blindness after saying a prayer for him. On Saturday, a girl in Gloucester prayed to Thomas and found that a bad headache went away. On Monday, a blind woman recovered her sight when she held a rag soaked in Thomas's blood against her eyes.

A shrine for Thomas

Ill and disabled pilgrims flocked to Canterbury. There, in the cathedral, the monks made a shrine for Thomas's body. They put his coffin inside a tomb made of marble. It had two holes on either side so that people could reach in and kiss the coffin. They also mixed drops of Thomas's blood with water and sold it to the pilgrims in tiny bottles made of tin.

Before long, miracles were happening every day. Mad people recovered their senses after drinking the water. Paralysed men walked home after a single drop. Children recovered from fevers as soon as the water passed their lips.

Many of these people left signs of their cure. The shrine was

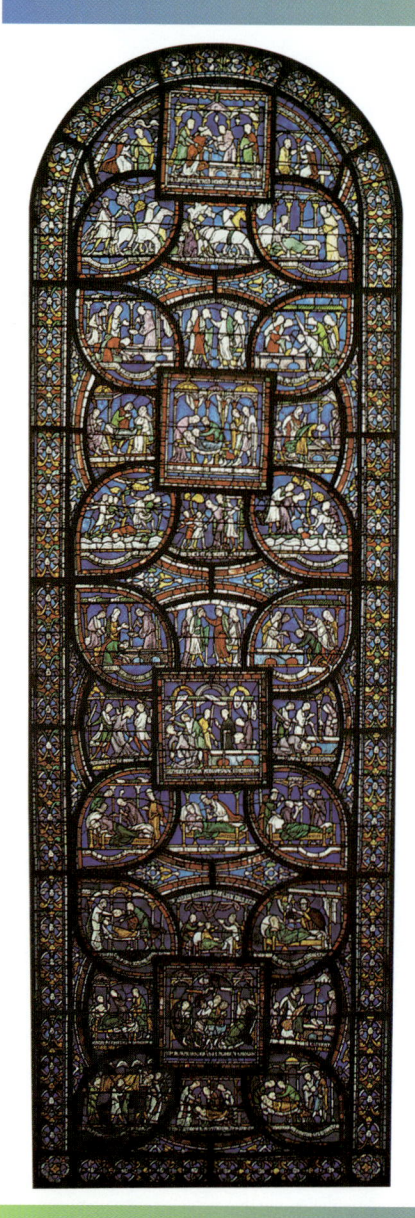

This stained glass window is in Canterbury Cathedral. It was made about 50 years after Thomas's murder. It is called a 'miracle window' because it shows some of the miracles that were said to have happened in his name. On the page opposite, one of the miracles is shown in three scenes.

Six boys are throwing stones at frogs in the River Medway, near Rochester. See if you can find the frogs jumping out of the river, and the stones which the boys are carrying in their coats. One of the boys, Robert, falls face first into the river.

Two of the boys rush to tell Robert's parents.

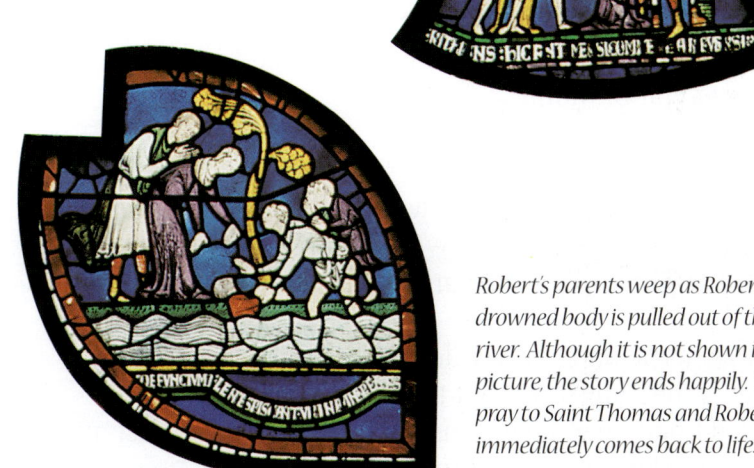

Robert's parents weep as Robert's drowned body is pulled out of the river. Although it is not shown in the picture, the story ends happily. They pray to Saint Thomas and Robert immediately comes back to life.

soon surrounded by crutches that their owners no longer needed. A boy with stomach pains coughed up a tapeworm after drinking the water, and left it hanging by the shrine.

News of the miracles reached the Pope. In 1173 he declared that Thomas was a martyr saint. As a result, the number of pilgrims rose still further. Within a few years of the murder, more than a thousand pilgrims were visiting the shrine every single day. Many of them left precious gifts, and soon the shrine was covered with plates of solid gold, and with diamonds, emeralds and rubies.

King Henry's penance

King Henry himself became a Canterbury pilgrim. Everyone blamed him for Thomas's murder and expected God to punish him for it. In 1173 it seemed that this was happening. Henry's sons rebelled against him, and the King of Scotland declared war on him.

Henry was in France when this happened. He returned immediately to England and went straight to Canterbury. As you have read (page 4), he walked barefoot to the cathedral, prayed at Thomas's shrine and was whipped by eighty monks.

He was immediately rewarded with a miracle. Within 24 hours, a messenger arrived to tell him that the King of Scotland had been taken prisoner the day before, just after the monks had finished whipping him. Shortly after this, his sons ended their rebellion, and Henry was safe again.

Lasting fame

As the years went by, the name of Thomas Becket became famous all over Europe. The monks who had known Thomas wrote dozens of books about him. Artists painted hundreds of pictures of the murder. Churches were renamed after him. Thousands of statues, stained glass windows and carvings kept his memory alive. The most famous book of the Middle Ages, *The Canterbury Tales* by Geoffrey Chaucer, is about a group of pilgrims riding to Canterbury to visit Thomas's shrine.

Task: miracles or make-believe?

Look at the pictures on pages 44–45.

1 In your own words, describe the miracle that is shown in the pictures.

2 Can you think of another explanation of how Robert recovered?

3 Why do you think that people explained it as a miracle rather than in the way you have?

You decide – saint or troublemaker?

1. Divide a page into three columns. Write these headings at the top of each column: Martyr, Confessor, Holy Man.

    a Now look at page 41. Under your three headings, copy down the meanings of the three kinds of saint: Martyr, Confessor and Holy Man.

    b Look at the statements below. In your three columns, write down anything about Thomas which makes you think he was that kind of saint.

    c Now write down anything about Thomas which makes you think he was *not* that kind of saint.

    - He was murdered after years of defending the Church against Henry's attempts to control it.
    - Miracles started to take place when people prayed to him after his death.
    - He earned a lot of money and spent it on good food, fine clothes, horses and presents.
    - He refused to obey King Henry on many occasions.
    - He gave up all luxuries when he became an Archbishop and started living by strict religious rules.
    - He was declared a traitor by a court of nobles and went into exile in France rather than accept their verdict.
    - He excommunicated bishops and nobles who challenged his authority.
    - He wore a prickly hair shirt to punish himself in the eyes of God.

2. When you have completed your three columns, use them to help you write three paragraphs.

    a Start the first paragraph with these words: *Thomas Becket can be called a saint because …*

    b Start your second paragraph with these words: *There were some things about Thomas Becket which were not saintly …*

    c Start your third paragraph with these words: *My opinion is that he was …* Then continue the paragraph with *I think this because …*